Every Little Girl

Janella McRae

Every Little Girl

I want to dedicate this book to my son Nicholas who is my world. I would not have made it this far without you son.

To all the women in my life who I look up to that inspires me everyday with their strength, light, and love.

To all the little girls that are reading this even if they don't hear this every day from anyone. Look yourself in the mirror and tell yourself you are:

- *BEAUTIFUL*
- *SMART*
- *STRONG*
- *YOU CAN DO ANYTHING IN THIS WORLD*

I AM LOVED

I AM HEALTHY

I AM SMART

I AM STRONG

I AM CREATIVE

I HAVE FAITH

I BELIEVE IN MYSELF

I AM JOYFUL

I AM CONFIDENT

I CAN DO ANYTHING

I AM BEAUTIFUL

I AM FEARFULLY AND
WONDERFULLY MADE

Made in the USA
Middletown, DE
17 November 2019